Munted

adjective NZ informal

1. in a state of disastrous disintegration; broken or ruined.

by Kate Slatter

Copyright © 2023 by Kate Slatter
Published by Kate Slatter
https://linktr.ee/slatterbooks

All rights reserved.
This book or any portion
thereof may not be reproduced
or used in any manner whatsoever
without the express written permission
of the publisher except for the use of
brief quotations in a book review.

ISBN: 978-0-6459498-0-3
Cover illustrations by Oscar Slatter
Internal illustration by Kate Slatter

Typesetting by Rack and Rune Publishing
rackandrune.com

Contents

Preface	5
Don't Be That Way	7
Words	11
I've Got a Golden Ticket	15
B.I.N.G.O.	21
Out of Touch	27
You Can't Stop the Music	31
My Favourite Things	37
Army of Me	43
Crazy	47
The Bare Necessities	53
Something is Not Right with Me	59
Spring, Spring, Spring	63
Time After Time	67
I'm a Fantastic Wreck	71
Material Girl	75
Shake it Out	81
My Girl	87
50 Ways to Leave Your Lover	91
Mr Blue Sky	97
Song list	101

Preface

This book is a gift.

Those of you who have experienced loss of this magnitude will recognise yourself in these pages.

For those of you supporting someone grieving, here you may find a way forward where there seems to be none.

Beautiful, funny, and painful to read, Kate brings to life the awful, yet somehow liberating, truth that 'the only way out is through'.

- Bec Wellard
(friend, neighbour, gestalt therapist)

Don't Be That Way

In April, we lost our beautiful Oscar to suicide. He was sixteen years old and amazing. His choice was a personal decision made by him. We have no blame for anyone, and we desperately avoid what ifs. Our life as we knew it has vanished, and we are in a new existence, without Oscar, and we miss him.

This blog is because, almost as soon as Oscar left, some things became incredibly valuable and some became completely irrelevant. Friends and family became our main tether to this alternate reality. Posting on Facebook became redundant. Chips – important. Wearing correct clothes – un-important. Time has almost no relevance.

I expect this will not be a fun blog to read, although some of the things we are experiencing ARE funny in a blackish sort of way. It is really more of a creative exercise for me to remind me of what is still good and likeable in a new reality that I would really rather not be needing to learn. It is a way to let our friends and family and people who we have forced to be our friends and family in the last month and a half, know how we are going (you still have to call and text and visit – this does not let you off the hook).

It will only be chronological in the fact that I am posting things at different times in an order that only goes forward. This is not through design and my posts are about what we are finding about ourselves, what we are feeling, and what enables us to survive. This is not the way we want to be. Nothing is how we want it. This is how we are.

Words

When Oscar left, we had to tell our family and friends. It sucked. We took turns, and had to psych ourselves up for each phone call. We didn't know what to say. Our families and friends didn't know what to say. NOBODY knows what to say. Here is a good tip.

SAY ANYTHING. Say, "I don't know what to say." Say, "I'm sorry." Say, "What can I do? I don't know what to do but tell me and I will do that." Say, "I feel totally inadequate but I am here for you." Say, "Fuck."

What NOT to do. Say nothing. Using the excuse that you don't know what to say, to allow yourself to say nothing, is a pussy move. It is hard to know what to say. It is hard to imagine losing your child. It's really hard to know what is going to help. It's frightening to know that something like this can happen to someone you know, to you. But what really sucks is being us. The family left behind.

Telling yourself you are not saying anything because you don't want to upset us is not correct. We are already pretty upset. I don't think we are going to feel worse because you remind us that Oscar is gone. We haven't forgotten. And not saying anything at all has the effect of making our reality that much harder to accept. We are already isolated and floating around like General Zod, stuck in the phantom zone in that dumb piece of mirror. All of our ties are broken. All of our future plans are gone. Who we are has had a huge chunk ripped out of it – possibly our virtual stomachs, if that hollow that we feel is them. We see the world and we do not want any part of it.

To survive, we need you. Your words, no matter what they are, are little ties that pull us back to this new reality. Every single text – and texting is good, because even though we want to know that you know Oscar is gone, sometimes we actually cannot talk – every single call, card, letter, email, hug, hand hold, pat on the shoulder, smile, tear, joke, story, food item left at our door, plant, certificate… every single point of contact is helping us survive. Even though we still don't know what to say. And you don't know what to say.

Sometimes you will say the wrong thing. We have heard lots of wrong things. Some really harsh ones too. People share stories of loss that are worse than ours – that doesn't make us feel better, by the way. People talk about us moving away. Were we leaving? We didn't realise. People say some shocking things, but that is STILL better than saying nothing. Because people say anything because they care. So when we hear a really weird statement come out of someone's mouth, we just ignore the words and translate it into "I love you," because that is what they are really saying.

Don't be scared to say something. We are scared that you won't.

Say anything.

I've Got a Golden Ticket

Yes. Gene Wilder as Willy Wonka was scary and that grandpa was gross. Sorry. It makes sense. Read on.

When Oscar left, there were a whole bunch of conventions, utterly meaningless to us as a family, that we had to discuss because it was assumed we would do them. We had to navigate a farewell for Oscar that felt like us, and felt like him. We are not religious. We do not read the paper. We don't bury bodies and we don't do drama.

The list went on… We don't want a fancy coffin, though finding out that upgrading a coffin or boosting the service at the crematorium is a thing, and that it is someone's job to sell those things to you in your moment of disintegration, is an eye opener.

We don't wear black. We didn't want to touch Facebook with a ten-foot pole. We find priests creepy. We don't go to church.

What we DO do, and do well, is certificates. People wanted to know if they could donate to

Black Dog, or any other group to help other people. At that point, I remember thinking "Other people? Who cares about them? WE need help," and our best pro survival tip was born.

When we sent out the invites to Oscar's farewell, we mentioned at the bottom that if people wanted to give a gesture of support, we would love to receive certificates for future activities or interactions we could share with them. We encouraged handmade, and suggested picnics, meals, outings to galleries... anything at all, that meant that when we were alone, as would eventually happen, we could pick a certificate and make a call and interact.

The certificates we received made me cry. We keep them in a bowl on the dining room table and shuffle through them when we need to fill the calendar because social engagement is key for us. We are still working through them but have so far received: chicken soup and bread delivered to our door, a family dinner, a drop in with guests bringing lunch, dinner delivery, phone calls of love, multiple pick-ups from work and being taken to lunch or coffee, a girls' weekend away, a handmade beanie... We have booked in another dinner, and a weekend away in the country including our dogs. We have many offers of stays, meals, camping trips, menu planning, dinner with strangers who are just happy to do something with us, elaborate picnics in the park, gallery visits, girls' day out, pony rides, games nights… Something so simple has made a massive difference to us. Our future disappeared and these things are there to build our new one on.

There are very few guides for what to do when someone's suicide leaves you behind. It is too shocking and scary. For some reason, although society has very clear procedures for if someone stubs their toe at work, we have no clear guide for when your child decides to leave for an alternate universe, just a bit earlier than you really were expecting.

We are told: Everyone's journey is different. It takes time. Be kind to yourself.

I will add – Ask for things. Asking for things is even easier than asking for help because asking for help makes you understand how fragile you are, and makes you feel like an object of pity, but asking for things makes people laugh, and it makes them happy because you are helping them understand what they can do to help, and they want to help! And it makes you happy because you get stuff, and that stuff is really more love packaged in all those certificates. And that love reminds you that you are also a person, with value, and importance to somebody else. And it is really, really important to be reminded.

We don't actually look at our certificates and dance around like Charlie's grandpa, but we do feel that lucky. We also most days get dressed, and even though we did all sleep in the same bed for about a week (including dog and cat), we mostly sleep in our own beds now.

Pyjamas, sharing the bed, looking like crap. Shit. It's possible we are Charlie's family. But if we are, we are them at that golden ticket part where everything is still total crap, but they feel hope.

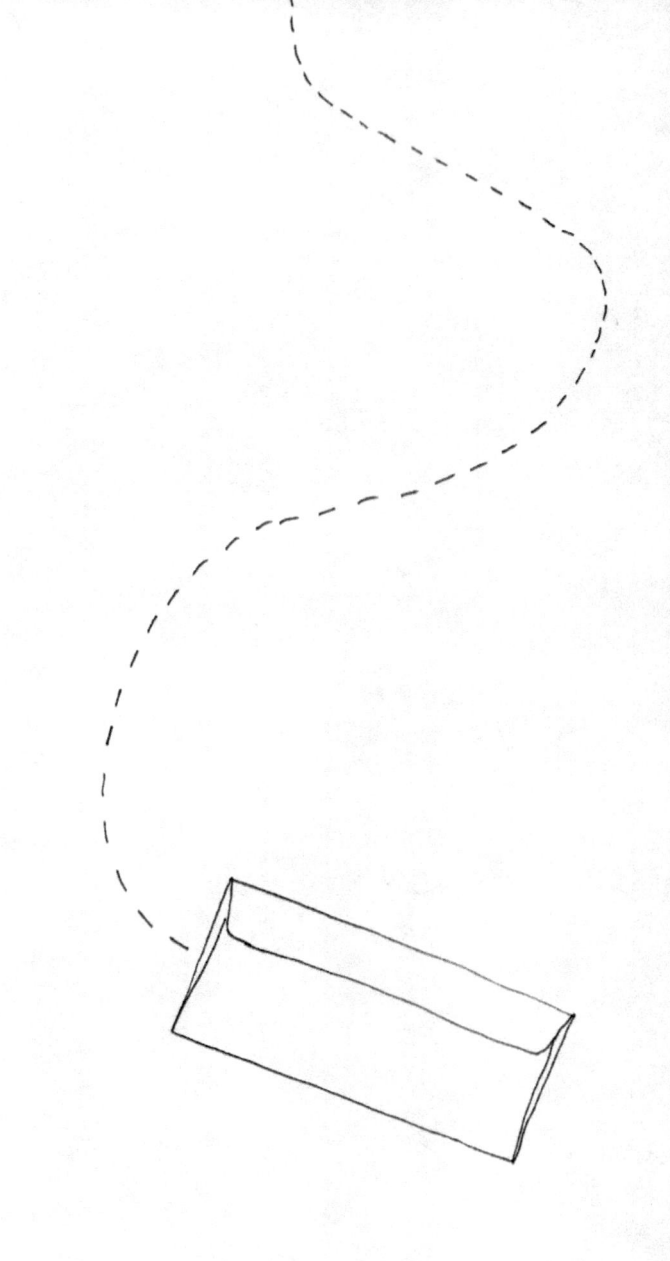

B.I.N.G.O.

A terrible song. If it has not yet been in a horror movie, it should be.

No one likes paperwork. We don't even do it when things are seemingly "OK." When they are not OK, automatically generated paperwork takes on a horror vibe, where it is sprung upon you when you are least prepared, packaged in something familiar yet off and wrong. I joked about making suicide survival bingo because there are so many shocking things that they become funny in the crazy laugh kind of way. People need warning. They need a buffer. They need protection.

Body

Where does your person's body go? You have to ask that. You have to talk on the phone with someone that has your body – and they are wonderfully sympathetic, however you still are not quite sure how long your person will be with them? When do they get cremated? Do they also burn the coffin? (Yes.) (And if so, why the upgrade?) How long does that take? When can we collect them? Where are they again? For us, Oscar's body was not Oscar. So we let him go in those first hours. But after a couple of weeks, we finally called the crematorium to ask, "Can we have him back?" "Oh, we just sent you a letter today (Friday). But we can talk on the phone about it, that's ok." Generous. Good training. An empathetic, practical touch.

In an urn, in a bear, in a lock of creepy hair...

So we collected Oscar. An awful, awful trip. But not as bad as the actual room where we got him. About the size of a dressing room and crammed – I mean crammed – with urns (are we Egyptian? why???), bears, boxes, crystals, pictures, paperweights (yes! this is a thing. Take your loved one to work and don't make people uncomfortable because they have no idea). It was like a nana's house where she's gone really sour, each item etched with a name and date of death and maybe a loving message. Were they real people? I don't know. Do people actually get that far along that they are in pick-up mode, and are then won over by the cuteness of a bear, and go, "Hang the expense! Let's get the bear!" because it is shoved in their face? Is there a marketing strategy? Were we perhaps in a storeroom because the serious room was booked and we had chosen the budget option? The room was so full of items that we were huddled together on one side of a desk with bears practically brushing our backs and urns at our elbows, and hunched together, we signed our paperwork and collected our son. It was truly so awful that I remember we did smile and shake our heads at each other in disbelief.

Not a package

At the end of a very long week, about four weeks on, we came home to a package notification. We were all exhausted but, having started to receive letters and small packages from people, one of us offered to go down and collect it for the rest. A little treat. A small distraction on a knackering Friday. Our package was Oscar's death certificate. Something no parent, no person, should ever have to see, let alone get in a moment of hopeful anticipation. One of those moments where you think, "Oh wait, no, THIS is the worst part, I thought I could not feel worse, but wait, I can."

gmail

My phone, with its loving texts and emails and pictures from people checking in, is so important to me that I once woke in the night with my hand cramped up where I had fallen asleep clutching it to feel when a msg would come through. I walk to work still checking it in the last few blocks, for something to get me through another couple of hours. I touch it constantly on my desk. I re-read emails that tell me I am a good parent. I scroll up and down the messages and read names to remind me of my friends. On the way to work one day I checked my gmail to find an auto-generated email survey request from the funeral home asking for my feedback on their service for the late Oscar. They asked me to be as frank as possible because that is really helpful to them. This was a crazy laugh moment. Just because you can DO auto-generated email surveys, is it possible that a funeral home may not be the best type of business to take that road? Maybe a more personal touch, like a phone call…? And frankly – how much repeat business are they expecting?

Oscar's accounts

Some things, we have still not had the strength to do. I have to call Centrelink and tell them Oscar has left, so they can tell Medicare and we stop getting Medicare letters for Oscar. I know I can do a form online and post it. In theory, I can do that. In reality, I start to and my mind wanders off. We have to shut Oscar's bank account. To do that we get to take his death certificate to the bank. We have to get a JP to verify that we are Oscar's parents and that his death certificate is genuine and take that signed paperwork along also. We have to be together. I feel sorry for whatever teller we get that day. I cancelled his phone plan. Although I clearly explained the reason for doing this, my telemarketer still kept asking if I was sure I did not want to retain the number for further use, as it would be terminated and I would no longer have access to it once I shut the account. I explained again that Oscar had self-terminated and that we would not be needing the number. They finally let me cancel the phone. His licence, his gym pass, his pool card, his student ID. Each one requires attention. Each one is a knife in your guts to tackle.

Look out for b.i.n.g.o. Be vigilant. Forewarned is forearmed.

Out of Touch

Hall and Oates are one of my favs but I have to admit to a dunderchief moment when I looked at the lyrics to this song. They were singing about souls? But also time. And being out of touch. And out of time…

We have many stressors now. A whole new world of things to feel in regards to grief, loss, trauma, and more grief, loss and trauma, and triggers when you drive by school, or the gym, or the supermarket, or leave the house, or go to bed at night or wake up.

A surprise stressor is time.

Grief takes time. We hear that a lot and it is true. But we thought it just meant that it is going to take a long time for us to understand our new world. We didn't realise it meant grief TAKES time. Highjacks time, beats it up and leaves it terrified in the corner. So when we look at the time, or see time passing, we get to share that fear.

Each morning we wake up. We get to experience the re-boot of our brains, to remind us that Oscar is not here. Then we see what state the rest of our bodies are in that day. Can we go to work and school? Are we feeling anything at all? How is our stomach? Will we throw up? Do we have a headache? All the while, the clock is waiting for us, putting pressure on us to perform in the normal way. To get dressed, eat breakfast, leave the house at the right time to beat the traffic. Get to work before nine. Stay all day. Leave at five. And you are afraid. I hate the clock now. I hate time. Because some days you cannot do it. And then you are terrified because you think, if not today, what about tomorrow? What about next week?

But you are also angry because time is made up! We operate to a nine-to-five schedule which makes very little sense once your world has been shattered. But the pattern is there in your head and you feel incredibly pressured to get back to that schedule, to perform in the way you have been conditioned to. Our biggest issue, asides from the huge gap where Oscar is not, is that demand to conform to time.

We are told by everyone – grief takes time, it's only been two months, you are doing so well… But the undercurrent of that is, "You still have to go to work." "You are paid to do a job so you need to do it." Or, "Why aren't you at school? You have to go to school." So we have verbal support, but non-verbal (and verbal! so awesome) anti-support because society is not geared for big sadness. There's not enough time for that.

Some mornings, watching the clock, and understanding that I need to stay home to support another person, leaves me in tears of frustration, panic and fear. I love my job. I love my daughter more. The relief I feel when I just steal a tiny bit of time for us, and maybe go to work at eleven, instead of nine, is immense. That is two hours to ensure sanity for that day. To give me time to ask for help, to organise care, to breathe.

We are both lucky to have incredible employers who have allowed us time to try and grasp just the edges of our new world. But time is ticking, and eventually, the morning will come when we are expected to present at nine and stay till five. To function in the expected manner. I feel that fear every day.

So we are out of touch and out of time. Outside of society and trying to conform but so awkward and broken that we do not really fit. Grief does take time. But you don't get any more time to replace it.

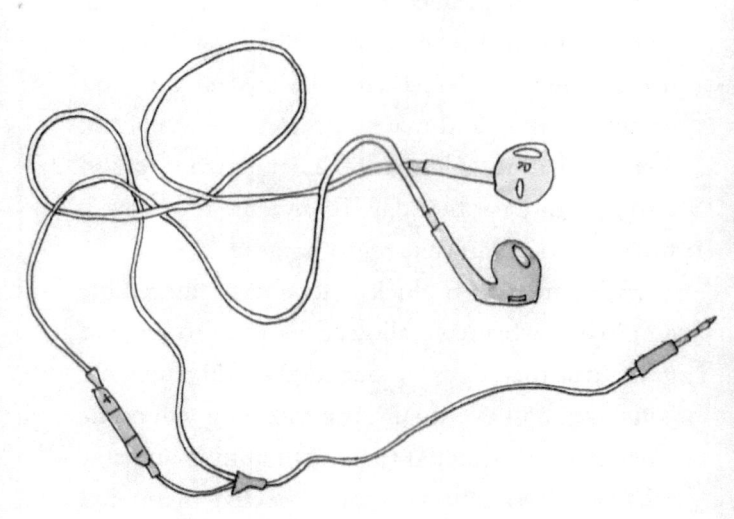

You Can't Stop the Music

Now you have that song AND image in your head, though all you did was read the words. So simple, yet so effective.

I love music and often have a theme song/album/playlist for the day. My memories are linked with songs. Before Oscar left, my taste was running to a mix of disco and 80s pop. I would play music while we got ready for school and the songs would get us to work and into the day.

Oscar loved music and had a huge, eclectic playlist. Thorough as always, he knew the reason behind stories, the influences of the artist, any contention about the song, and he was charmed at funny, clever lyrics. He would play me songs in the car when we were together and explain why he liked them or give me random facts about them.

We inherited Oscar's playlist, downloaded onto our phones, and have gradually modified it to suit our tastes. My daughter has a completely different list now than mine, and for each of us, that is Oscar's playlist. A lot of the time it is hard to listen to, but once in a while it just reminds you of Oscar and how lively and interested he was in things, and that is good. But music from before is harder to listen to as you can so clearly remember doing a million activities with all of us and those songs. Nothing seems relevant. And it does not make you happy.

In the days that followed Oscar's decision, our house was filled with people. When they asked what we needed, we said, you. Please come over. And everyone did. A full house means music, but it was impossible to find the right thing in our library and Oscar's playlist was too sad and too hard. We needed new songs, but Oscar was the person in our family who mostly sourced them. We needed music that meant strength and happiness and joy in crap times but that was still cool! Cue Marvin Gaye, George Benson, Daft Punk, David Bowie… We went 60s and 70s, with a dash of 80s and a couple of 2017s (how does that work?) and found that it was comforting and good.

I now have a mix that I cannot work out a

name for, but it is definitely Oscar's and ours. I fiddled with it for a couple of weeks, testing it on the others, adding and rejecting songs, finding new songs I had not heard and revisiting old songs. It is mixed with songs that have strong but recent memories with Oscar – a trip to Seattle and our theme song for that, or one from a movie we all loved. But it is high in older music, some from my own playlists, that we all knew, some only I remember from growing up, and a couple of new ones that just fit. It is chronological; for one song I will forever think of my mum cleaning the stove, in preparation for Oscar's farewell celebration (side note – having the stove cleaned was something I said frequently when people asked what they could do for us. It took four days, but eventually, my mum did it. We also asked for toilet paper and bottles of sparkling water). It moves through my own memories, our time as a family together, and then adds some of Oscar's songs, finishing up with a couple from his playlist and mine.

This playlist means strength and survival to me. It reminds me that even in the beginning we were determined not to go under. Even though for weeks I would play it in the car and simultaneously sing and cry all the way to work and all the way home. I totally still do that, but sometimes, it also makes me feel tough and proud. When people say there are tools to help you with grief, add music. Although your old world is lost, and you feel there is nothing to hold on to, you really can't stop the music. What you can do, is use it to carry feelings and memories of your person so you will always be able to find them.

My Favourite Things

We are still not dancing, and no-one has the nun haircut. But concentrating on very simple, achievable things is good. Simple is all we can tackle. We cannot even promise actions for tomorrow, but search every day for something – anything – to help drag ourselves into the world. No big changes is the rule we are told, but we needed some new *things* to focus on.

Raindrops on Roses

Our yard is consistently half-assed. It is a huge, rambling jungle of out-of-control vines, chickens, dogs, frogs and piles of rubbish. We had been attempting to claim some order and installed four garden beds to fill. We sit inside and look out over the empty beds. One now contains a rose plant from one of Oscar's friends. We see that every day. Another contains a collection of pansies, all different colours, that took up an afternoon of our time, outside in the sun, focusing on the colours and the activity.

Whiskers

We got a dog to sleep on our beds. He is handsome, gentle, dorky and kind. Our dog loves him. We love him. He is a new thing in the house that we can care for and talk to and learn about.

Salt and Vinegar Kettles

Chips really need a mention as we eat BAGS and BAGS of potato chips. It's awesome.

Woollen Mittens

It is winter. We are freezing and shock also makes you feel numb. We've collected all of our cosy blankets and we cuddle on the couch, binge watching TV. We bought a special (totally wrong) faux fur blanket called a pelage (a real word, I looked it up. It means fur/hair/wool of a mammal which is even grosser). It is supposed to be polar bear I think, but we try not to think about that.

Brown Paper Packages

We buy ourselves small treats. Cocoa powder that makes red hot chocolate because there is beetroot in it. Magazines. Sourdough bread. Gifts for each other that mean "Good work for making it through the day" and "I love you."

Ponies

Nope.

Apple Strudels

Eventually, we ran out of frozen meals and we had to start cooking again. We started with roast dinners so we would have a huge tray of cheesy veggies, potatoes and gravy and meat to last a few days. We made apple crumble. We made more roast dinners. Cooking is still a challenge but mostly because we are just so *tired*. It does make you feel better to produce your own meal of any type. More because you can include veggies than because you want to be a kitchen master. We started to get scurvy from all the pies so really the cooking was another move towards survival…

Doorbells

We still like visitors but now you mostly have to ask them to come. People don't just rock up anymore and it is a bit harder to call and say – we need you.

But you can also call and say – "We are coming over to you," and that works as well. Bring food and drink. They cannot refuse you.

Schnitzel

You can get a pub tea to go! For when you cannot cook and you want your pub schnitzel and veg but you are also wearing layers of pyjamas, terrible hair and have not got the energy to even pretend to be polite.

Wild Geese

We bird watch. We have magpies and kookaburras, regent bower birds and fantails. We have ravens and goshawks, rosellas and king parrots. Now we feel that the birds are dropping in to say hi and to cheer us up. We are always looking for them and it takes the focus out of our heads and off into the sky and trees.

Satin Sashes

After Oscar left, we shopped. We bought clothes and jackets. A blue velvet lounge. Fancy food, haircuts and hair colours. Anything that could be used as a tactile distraction, that made us feel different and presentable (once we stopped wearing pyjamas). We bought bags of bath bombs. I bought perfume so I had a new scent for the new world. Our credit card is totally maxed out. It's ok. It got us through to now.

No Flakes

I brutally culled my contacts list to people who are brave enough to spend time with us. Those who came to our house in the first, terrible days. Those who called, texted and made contact in any way at all. I am also accumulating new people who are equally bold and have come into colour and focus for us in this new reality. They have stepped out of the grey blur and into our lives with kindness, honesty and care.

Winters That Melt Into Spring

It is winter. Metaphorically and actually. Can't say that I am loving it, but I am sure there is a message of hope here. Time will tell.

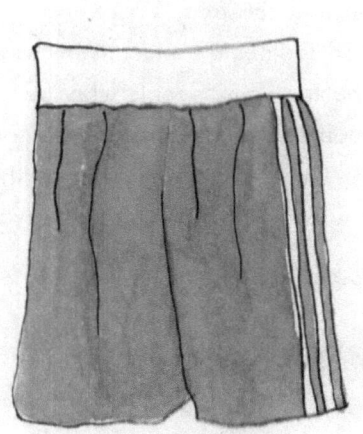

Army of Me

This song is loud, feisty and mad. This is pretty much how we feel many days. We hate this world, we hate other people and we hate each other.

It is strange to feel so angry for so long. It doesn't feel like you, but it is you. We seem to be able to coast along and do what needs to be done, but then the anger comes and you cannot shake it. Previously, I would have called myself a positive person. Cynical, but positive. Whatever happened I knew I could Pollyanna the shit out of any situation. Lying in bed at night, after a horrible day, I would think, everyone's home, everyone's alive, we can do something else tomorrow… But there is no fix for this. Everyone is NOT alive. There's no lesson to learn. There's no picking up the pieces. There's no making up, and saying sorry, and making changes, and trying harder. There's nothing.

And that's really what you hate. You are helpless, through no action of your own. It's so unfair! And then you are embarrassed to sound like a whiny person, and then you are angry again because you are embarrassed. And then just angry. Sometimes, conveniently, some poor idiot says the wrong thing or is rude or ignorant or just exists in your sphere and you can be angry at them. You can put a reason to the mad and the relief! But eventually you realise you are being unfair and you are left with the mad all to yourself.

Because we are all different, we find ourselves in different mental spaces at different times and it is hard to find the patience and care that we previously had for each other. We are worn down. There are no more reserves to be gently accepting and to be the person who makes the food while the other two lie on the couch, under the pelage, watching endless Netflix, brain cells flickering out with each episode. And it is frightening to watch each other just stop, and not be able to do anything at all, and to allow that to happen, because there is nothing else you can do. But we have to do it. We argue and yell at each other (from prone positions lying in front of the fire). We storm out of the house (ok – that was me). But at the end of the day, we only have each other and we have to still say, "We're going to survive. This is shit but we have each other."

We are fighting years of conditioning that say being angry is bad, or wrong, or needs to be fixed. We are learning a new type of acceptable behaviour and feelings that are exclusive to our tiny family.

I am quite sure that exercise is the key here. I imagine myself in a montage of fitness, not only working out my anger but becoming incredibly buff in the process and wearing those shiny boxing shorts and plaits, even though I have short hair, and don't own those shorts. I try to visualise our family going to the gym. Very difficult. We could walk but it is so cold, and dark, and night time by the time I get home from work and… I know that is what we need to do, but paired with the anger is a torpid inability to take action.

Time will sort this. Accepting that also allows me to not be mad that I am not buffing up yet. Sometime in the future, I am there in my boxing shorts, hopefully less angry, possibly buff. Expanding on this I can see the three of us in those Royal Tenenbaum tracksuits. Not jogging, because jogging is wrong, but perhaps attempting some sort of fitness regime which accommodates the wearing of those tracksuits. I wouldn't hate that.

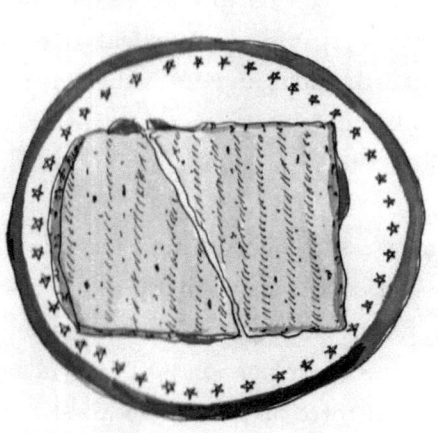

Crazy

So many versions and all of them sad. It's too bad that we are geared to find routine comforting, as this makes the experience of big grief that much more challenging. We now know that it will take what feels like forever to grasp our Oscar is gone from this world. We know that exhaustion stripping away our filters is a norm for us. We can try to remember to forgive ourselves as we have one more lame ass dinner of toasted sandwiches or popcorn (with cheese – dairy!). Time has brutally taught us a little, and we say to people, "We're doing as best we can." Our newest participant into this gruelling experience, and one who is disturbingly enticing, is crazy.

Every move we make, and thought we have, presents us with a choice. And by trying to remember who we are, or more to the point, who we now want to be, we can try to make a choice that gels with that. At first we made little choices. I have blue hair. I have random clothes, and I mix them up shamelessly. My daughter got a haircut. We got the dog. Small differences that have few consequences. Sometimes I am aware I look hectic, and I don't care. Because what does it matter? Previously, I would have reigned myself in a little, to fit in, to keep people comfortable. But what good did that do me?

Now the universe has taken a big shit onto our lives, and we are helpless to reverse it, we question everything. And in questioning, we become aware of just how much we do that makes very little sense. And we can feel ourselves doing a sort of Matrix reveal where we start to feel there are other possibilities. Enter crazy – or is it? And there are so many options!!!

Most horrible is that our brains are still processing, still rewriting tracks of thought in our heads. So many times a week, you think to text or call Oscar, or you look forward to seeing him, because you miss him, and you try to work out when he is going to be home. This takes about a second. Then the current reality thoughts catch up with those, and there is a crash, and you are alone. You look back at that other track and think, "Can't I just stay there? Where's the harm? This world sucks balls anyway and I have no control and being a good person does not count for anything at all, and what am I doing here that makes any difference anyway?" At that point, you could just slide into insanity and go. You want to just forget.

Once you remember that he is not here, you sometimes try to visualise him somewhere else.

Where is he? Does he have a consciousness? Does he know what he did to us? Is he in that alternate reality, with a different version of us, has had his birthday and is romping his way towards the HSC, blissfully unaware of this shattered reality we are stuck in? Can we go there too? You want to be there. You certainly don't want to be here.

We question our choices of job, location, outlook on life (currently fairly low). Our marriage, our parenting…

And then we claw our way back by calling a friend or making food, or getting dressed and going to work or school. But at the same time our minds are howling WHY? Why are we doing this? I have not met any other parents surviving the suicide of their child. I am nervous to go to the support groups in case they are still wrecked ten years down the track – in case I see people who are clinging to this one hideous event, and that is all they are. I don't want that, but I can see how easily it could happen, and I am afraid.

I can't imagine a time when I will ever really want this world. We are waiting for time travel, or for aliens to take us all away. Global warming is too slow. Crazy seems quite accessible at this point.

Would it be crazy to pack up and move to

Scandinavia? (Yes – too cold.) What's wrong with selling everything and sailing away? Really – what's wrong with that? We don't have an answer except that it feels like running away. Which seems a little… chicken.

Sometimes it feels like all that is keeping us together is a desire not to be beaten. That and the fact that people keep telling us – and we tell ourselves – No Big Changes. We know we are not quite rational, but crazy says, "Who cares? Rational didn't win us any prizes so far." What we can see is that we are in the middle of this big grief, and it is not finished with us. It seems practical to stay put and see it through as long as we can bear it. And once we decide that, maybe we can take a bit of the crazy and use it to our advantage.

Because some of the things that we no longer care about, we will never care about again. And that's ok. Filterless conversation – something I thought I was already pretty good at – has become even more enjoyable. I spend less and less time in the middle ground of meaningless chatter. I like my ridiculous wardrobe. We eat whatever the hell we want. We are brutally honest with each other and our brave friends. This does not mean rude, it means truth: ugly, pretty, embarrassing, funny, sad. Crazy.

Once, when our daughter was quite young, she made an elaborate set up of dolls and toys. We were admiring it, and she said, "Wait – I'm missing a vile contestant!" Mystified, we waited to see who she would bring back. It was Barbie, and we realised she meant "Vital Component." Evidently, Barbie had a role to play. Privately, we still considered her vile because – Barbie! Crazy is a bit the same. A vile contestant that is integral to our grief.

The Bare Necessities

Maybe if this song was sung by Iorek Byrnison instead of Baloo, it would be a bit more appropriate for where we are at. But the gist is there. Along with shattering our reality, Oscar leaving destroyed how we see ourselves. We don't know who we are anymore. Losing Oscar has been so all-encompassing, it is hard to focus on anything but the essentials. Eat, sleep, make sure the three of us are ok (have not found a better word for this as ok does not really apply). But as we start to do things we used to, it becomes starkly obvious that some parts of us are gone forever.

We have lost how we see ourselves, how we talk about ourselves, our confidence in being an amazing, fun and fabulous family unit of four. When people ask, "How many kids do you have?" we don't know what to say. Watching parents with sons is unbearable, but you can't look away. You are watching a world you used to be part of. There might as well be a giant pane of glass in between you and those innocent parents, and you are an ancient crone looking back on a different life. At those times, the multiverse is very present. The feeling that you are in a separate bubble overlapping someone else's is SO strong. But it is entirely unattainable. You can't get over there.

Those craving the people we used to be are particularly difficult. You automatically go along with the role-play, because you are sorry for what Oscar has done and you are tired. In your numb state, you don't really care what is happening so if someone else calls the shots, that is easy. But as time passes, the play is more and more painful. We are not those people anymore. They are gone. And really, it is selfish for people to cling to that past you. It is entirely beyond your power to be that person because that person had Oscar and we don't.

Understanding that is not tragic, it is just fact. The new you is pared back to a sharp, stark collection of values and needs. The bare necessities. Even though we are not walking around with Oscar's loss primary in our thoughts, it is always there. One of the worst things we could imagine is our reality now. Small dramas are meaningless. Pettiness, rudeness and idiocy are intolerable. We are aliens, watching humans and confused at their actions. We crave kindness, courtesy, food, friends.

Honesty. Clear communication. Love. In the everyday world these things seem to be found in brief bursts only, but these are the only things that make sense to us. Reading this, you would think that we will now become amazing, gentle humans, considerate of others and full of compassion. Not.

Along with stark values, our numb feeling is replaced with a sort of detached efficiency. Because task completion is part of survival, we find it hard to be half-assed. Once noted, the task must be done, regardless of the impact on others. Then you move straight onto the next task. A cyborg of efficiency. No dithering, no fluff, no tolerance for lesser beings. Sometimes I wonder if I will change jobs? Will I get through the first year, or the first three years and find I am something new? But what would that be? ATO employee? HR termination consultant? Assassin?

Once again, our saving grace is our friends. And the key to these friends is acceptance. Our friends give us space to be whatever we are on that day. They are convinced that we are worthwhile people, that we have some value and even that we are fun! They do not demand a role from us. They do not avoid all mention of Oscar, as if by not mentioning him, we can just gloss over this unpleasant situation. They make plans with us, and give us something to look forward to. Our friends remind us of what we do have, and of the parts of us that are still there. They tell us their own stories, share their lives and make the world a bit more real.

We can't have Oscar. We're not really going to forget that. Sorry Baloo. But operating with just the bare necessities is maybe not so bad for now.

Something is Not Right with Me

Travelling is a better term than "ok" for what we are doing. Not a journey I would have chosen. Not many laughs. No going home. But travelling fits better than ok somehow, and it feels true. At this point in our travels, we are quiet.

Our guests have dropped off, through just having their own lives, or by our own direction. We are introspective, deciding how we feel, and working out who plays what parts in our family of three. We argue more. We sleep a LOT. We've tried (ok this is me again) to stop asking the others if they are going commit suicide while I am out. This is a real fear.

We still have our support crews and still undertake excursions and activities to hold our attention. We go out to dinner. We paint the house. We engage. But something is not right. If we have to be in this world – as it gradually becomes apparent that we do as, disappointingly, the aliens have failed to arrive for us – we cannot just quietly slide into it. Something is drastically wrong, though it is not apparent when meeting us. Oscar's choice has changed us. And we need people to know. The urge to share the loss of Oscar with this world is very strong. If we are going to stay here – we will stay on our terms, and those terms are acknowledging Oscar. His life, his choice, our loss, the destruction of our plans and fantasies and the brutality of the present.

But how to tell people? There's not many conversational segues to suicide. People are not really keen to discuss it and it doesn't often pop up in conversation. That's what you tell yourself. And it is what people assume. But I am making and finding a different truth.

We think our news is cruel and hurtful. That we will sound like crazy, self-focused people, reliving our loss again and again. In fact, almost the opposite is true. I started with my contractors at work. People I always felt happy to see. Not mentioning Oscar feels like we are hiding something, not being honest. So as soon as I saw them, once I was back at work, I told them. Suicide is shocking, but people are kind. I got and continue to get hugs, queries on how we are travelling, a kiss (hair-dressers), hot chips (winning). People are able to deal with your news. They don't hate you for sharing. The amount of people who have had their lives scarred by suicide is surprising. But you would never know any of this, without taking the first step of opening up the conversation. And then suddenly, with those few words, they become part of your world.

There is so much conversation on preventing suicide, seeking help, speaking out, offering support. But once that horse has bolted, silence reigns (unintentional horse pun). If anything, more energy seems to be poured into prevention and awareness. But those already left behind are in a limbo of failure. We didn't stop it. Our person cannot seek help because they are already gone. Is there even a name for us? Victims? Left-overs? Both seem unpalatable. Surely we can think of a stronger, more kick ass name for our survival? If we had a name, maybe we could find each other? And then maybe the language of how to talk about suicide – after the fact – could become more mainstream.

Perhaps this desire to speak out is a just a stage of our grief, so we will now indulge in a frenzy of horror sharing, shocking grocers, check-out people and innocents waiting at traffic lights with us, and then maybe we will get past it? Maybe not. As usual, we just don't know. But taking any action and following our instincts is what feels right. So we will be talking. About Oscar. About suicide. About how something is terribly, horribly not right with us.

Spring, Spring, Spring

yaaaay….. Weather changes are great markers for memory, emotions and thoughts. Although we are still feeling quiet, we are also feeling spring. It is painful and good at the same time (a bit like this song). A mix which I think is ours forever now.

Spring intrudes with warmer days, sun, flowers… there is really nothing crap about it. It is a good lesson in reminding us that going outside and being in the world is a way to survive. You don't see change lying under the pelage. But always we are careful to remember that this is a different spring, an alternate place. There are still so many traps to be mindful of as you work out who you will be.

As talking about Oscar's absence in our lives and talking about suicide in general becomes just a part of the conversation, not THE conversation, we find there are many opportunities for change for us and we don't want to miss those doors. Every conversation and decision is an opportunity to make a choice, to make an ethical stand, to express an opinion, or just to listen and hear something you had not noticed previously. At this point in time, with the loss of Oscar at the forefront of people's minds, we can become anything we want with very little social pushback. It is exhilarating and exhausting. At the end of the day we are wrecked. I wonder if we will ever not be tired.

It is fun though. Our loose boundaries, loss of filters and mental fatigue result in a "Why not?" attitude which means you ask for things or take actions where you may previously have given yourself time to procrastinate and dither. We know that time is an illusion. There might not be a tomorrow, so if we want to do something or want something to happen, we need to do it straight away. We're not Amazons though, so dragging our bodies along the path of self-discovery will still take some time.

I did get a gym card. It is shiny. I have not gone into the gym though. Driving by the pool, I see that it is open. We get a box of seasonal veggies from a food co-op fortnightly. In order to maintain some standards, we will not be buying Birkenstocks, but we do discuss more vegetarian meals. Spring is weaselling in, despite our grief.

It is strange to just be smiling because there is sunshine. And confusing. Because in one way it feels like mere seconds since Oscar has gone, and in another it feels like years and years. We have tried to accept each feeling, and each day as it happens, in order to let our brains understand what this reality is. It is not fun. Some days are very harsh, but we do it. Sometimes you scream with the wrongness and injustice of this place we are in. Sometimes it is just unbearable. But we are still here. And I am proud of us. I hope we get to do something with this strength that we are building.

We used to watch Oscar and wonder how the world would cope when he grew up and really entered it as an adult. He was such a force and constantly surprised us with the way he saw things and how he questioned pretty much everything. We won't get to see that now, but we're keeping the attitude. It's ours. An already contrary family, we are now even more so because we are surviving this nightmare and we will continue to do so. It's Spring. And we are waking up. And I almost feel the same sense of pity for the world that I used to when I imagined Oscar unleashed.

Time After Time

I used to sing this song in karaoke, a lifetime ago. It is very repetitive.

Currently, we are stuck in a loop. We go to work, go to school, eat, sleep (sort of) and we grind through the days without Oscar. The mere act of existence is a physical effort. There are still days when we wish we could just disappear. Luckily, we can express this to each other, and what follows is an equally exhausting series of activities which include outings, shopping, exercise, friend visits, and much sitting very close to each other in silence, so we are touching (or alternatively gripping quite tightly). We hug a lot more.

You try and find victories, try to see ways in which you are succeeding, ways that this world is positive, things to cheer about. And you sort of can. I swim now. We cut out kettle chips. Our house and yard are changing. We are still performing the expected actions of society. But most days, at some point, when you are alone, you are filled with devastation. There is no escaping this reality. And it is never going to be ok. Learning is repetition. Or repetition is learning. Whatever. What it means for us is that our brains constantly take us right back to the start of this alternate reality. So fun.

We are currently in a private and mostly silent hell where that night happens again and again. Dreams, flashbacks, many of the realisations that hit us in the first month as our shock wore off, we get to do again. It is hard to express this verbally, even though we thought we were doing pretty good with communication. In some ways it feels like a failure, like we are going backwards, even though we know we are not. When someone asks, "How are you going?" it is really difficult to say, "Horrible. I dreamed about Oscar last night and I can't get the images out of my head." Though as I write this, I realise that I had this exact conversation last week with someone. I guess it depends on the person.

You feel betrayed by life, stuck in this seemingly endless loop of sadness. And you don't want to remind people that life is not in fact linear – it is just a big messy scribble. Socially, silence on that matter is entirely acceptable, which is disturbing. You need energy to ignore other people's linear projections, but more importantly, you need energy to fight your own expectations of what you should be doing. To remember that there are no rules, no particular path, no right or wrong for your feelings. Though you desperately want the world to make sense in some way, it just doesn't. Though you want time to make things gradually feel better, that is not going to happen. Though you want your grief to progress in a line, with milestones and rewards along the way, that's also a no.

In karaoke, you think "Time After Time" is a safe option. You won't forget the lyrics. The range is easy. It's a bit of a nostalgic crowd pleaser. But once you start singing, you start to cringe every time the chorus approaches. It goes on and on and on.

At the moment, it feels like we are wading through cement. But we are resilient. And we have wonderful, understanding friends. And weirdly enough, in extremely brief glimpses, you still have hope. Possibly, there will be a time – after this time (or within, or concurrent – we're flexible) – with more interesting lyrics.

I'm a Fantastic Wreck

At last, a song I truly like.

It feels like our periods of introspection are longer and longer. Spaces of time where we just absorb our present existence without even trying to explain it. But the desire to make some sort of story is very strong. Despite all evidence to the contrary, you STILL try to make a tale that ends happily. Ha! No wonder so many people are miserable. The expectations fed to us as we grow in the world are ridiculous. There is no fairy-tale ending. You just have to find a way to like the mess you are in. Previously we considered ourselves lucky to be able to have kids – that's really lucky. It didn't occur to us that we would also be lucky to keep them. Who promised that? In the same way that no woman will ever tell you your vagina might fall out after a pregnancy or two, until it actually does – then everyone suddenly has a prolapse story to share – no-one reminds you to watch out for suicide. Though statistically it should be as common a conversation as any. But who really wants to be reminded of how many people we lose?

Unbelievably, we still have a desire to win, to triumph in some recognisable way. But if we were to try and do that based on social norms, having your child opt out so comprehensively puts you right out of the running. We are very, very lucky to have our daughter. Yet we are still stratospherically far from the people we see around us. We win at work and our daughter wins at school but, for a driving force – something to engage our interest and give us a reason to play this out, we need more. A new definition of winning – which really has nothing to do with winning and more to do with enjoying. Smiling. Laughing. Exploring. Some grand adventure, just for us. Tricky.

Because we are a broken family. We feel it when we drive by other families, or go out to dinner with just the three of us. We are a wreck. But can't a wreck be sort of fascinating? What about sunken ships? Abandoned houses. Tip shops. I like the idea of taking our wreck and making it something amazing. It may not look like anything that anyone else thinks is amazing. But it will be wonderful to us.

It's a messy process. And some days you really have to force it. We are doing a combo of accepting grief in its zillion guises while simultaneously taking life by the balls and squeezing really hard. And then sleeping. And then crying. Cooking. Painting. And then a bit more squeezing and maybe a kick or two. I am prickly at work, then bring banana cake for everyone. I'm trying not to label myself at this time because, if I did, I would have to settle for asshole. Or maybe, asshole with cake. That balances out, right?

Oscar is part of our life. We had him with us for seventeen years. Our daughter never knew life without him till now. And the way he left us has an impact that we need to weave into our now, to make it bearable. We can't hide it. We won't leave it behind after a certain amount of time. We will never not talk about him when we think of him. Instead, we will take the wreck he left us and make it part of ourselves. It's not pretty. But it is honest. It's been so hard to imagine a way to see ourselves that feels good. But this feels right. We may be broken but we can be fantastic wrecks.

Material Girl

It is harder and harder to think about our current life because the world without Oscar, the understanding that he is not here, feels so wrong, like such a huge mistake, that you cannot grasp it.

Our reality has split again. There is the now. It's almost Christmas. We've put up garlands and bought new fairy lights. We are cleaning out the house and gardening. Work, school, cooking, exercise… Overlapping this is the other world where you are paralysed with the loss of Oscar. How do you engage with now, when every minute holds a path to that other place? Every step into now holds a trap door to your loss, so even when you think you are doing it, you are broadsided by a birthday card, or a drawing, or a message of love in really bad handwriting. Do you put it all in a box? What do you label that? Oscar? Our old world? Old life? Which you no longer have?

There was a time where I thought I understood. I could look at the three of us and say, "This is the shape of our family." But now I find that there are only glimpses of this smaller picture, and often, I struggle to accept it. I feel that this is not helpful.

What stage is this? Is this why people always say, "I don't know how you are doing it?" because they thought I was always feeling this? Do we ever get a break? (I'm thinking no.)

The thing is, you know you have to understand, but you don't know how to. To let your child go. Who does that? How do you divvy up what to hold and what to release? Once, when I was nobly coping, I imagined giving our lives to Oscar like a beautiful, massive cloak. He could wrap himself up in it and fly off to wherever he is, with us always around him, holding him warm and safe. All our stories, dreams and love for him in a big colourful pelage of us. I like that image. And in fact, that is what a suicide does. He did take our lives with him at the same time as he took his. And if they are in the form of a wonderful, brilliant cloth of love, that's comforting (yes).

I have feelings of Oscar when I am swimming, or hear a particularly bad song that I know would have made him smile. They make me smile for a few seconds and I feel massive love for Oscar and that, maybe, he can feel it too. But then I have to get out of the water, or stop driving, and re-enter the now. And he is gone.

It feels like the material world is where we have to be, as if the only other option is to become crystal-toting recluses, constantly looking for signs that Oscar is still here. You can cherish those short moments when you just feel like he is with you, but you cannot seek them. Maybe in the future there will be a more gentle melding of the two, but for now it seems pretty stark. Person who still has a family, ability to afford food and a home, versus mentaller who stays in bed forever. Decisions decisions... How fortunate that Christmas is here and, once again, we get to find a way to make a minefield event into something meaningful for us. Cheers for that, Jesus.

We've booted Christmas day entirely and will be walking the dogs, snorkelling, swimming and feasting in the garden with our family of three humans, two dogs, one cat and six chickens. We're still making cinnamon rolls. We are organising careful small gatherings in the days around Christmas. We're expecting visitors. We are going to the zoo. It's going to be a shit Christmas. We all know that. But like Madonna, we are resilient and have the ability to change, even when we really, really don't feel like we can.

Oscar took our cloth with him, and we will work out what our new material looks like. Friends, family, food, garlands, glitter, gifts. Chickens, laughter, dogs in bed, plants, no pants, flowers, spiders and soda water. Ponds, paintings, mosaics and madness. If we have to be living in a material world, it's going to be a cloth of our own design. Very colourful. Definitely waterproof. Quite hard wearing. Possibly fire retardant...

Shake it Out

Florence, not Taylor. Out not off. And this is less of a description and more of a wish. There's nothing shiny about 2019. All the usual hopes, plans and ideas triggered by a new year are flat and featureless. I can say the words and look at holiday destinations but deep down it feels pointless and I really don't care.

I remember that I've been told things get better. They certainly look better. Our house is lovely. We have painted and moved dirt and brought in plants. Our space looks great. I am reminded of the many people who are beautiful, successful and amazing and who suddenly opt out and everyone is surprised. I don't want that for our house, but looking at the beauty and feeling nothing is worrisome. The same way I am suspicious of people with really clean houses – I worry that our very fun transformation is a picture masking a big fat nothing. Behind very beautifully potted plants. With a really good view.

Each time we make a colour choice, it is a fine balance between arty, fun, even edgy, and just a little bit too edgy. No one wants to be the purple lady (we all know one). We painted our lounge room floor seven times. Then added fish. I really love it. Even writing this makes it more comforting and sound sort of cool. But we might wake up next month and think, "What the…?" But ultimately I know, it's only paint. It just doesn't matter.

So how do we shake it out? We stay busy. Go to the beach. Be kind. Cook, though flavour is elusive. Each day, I choose to believe that it gets better, though there is no evidence to support this. And sometimes the grind of going through the motions leaves me in tears in a supermarket aisle. I concurrently hope that when we fly, our plane will fall from the sky, or that a large meteorite will strike earth, offering instant relief.

I can see that this is a sucky way to be. We need more shaking. I've shaken out haircuts entirely. I keep getting compliments which is confusing but heartening I guess. Who would have suspected that greying, Brady hair could trump my previous, glossy cuts? I shook out pants, but really because they just don't fit anymore – despite shaking out chips! We shook out a whole bunch of meat eating. Which has also led to some creative vegetarian cooking. I keep hoping for some sort of phoenix reveal of the New Us. A different description to Fucked. I'm not feeling it though. Fooled again by the concept that life is linear, and situations conclude tidily. There is no end for us and that is the difficulty.

A useful trick is to engage in things that do have a clear start and a finish, preferably with some sort of recognition at the end. I'm going back to uni – little quizzes, marks, passes and distinctions. Perfect! Though in the back of my mind, still meaningless. I'm doing it. And I will pretend it means something. We continue to renovate, which generates pictures of fun things people can compliment us on (do that, by the way). Our daughter has started Year 9. The year will pass and she will no doubt triumph. Or maybe she won't. And that's ok. The year will still pass.

I almost feel apologetic about feeling like this and sometimes don't bother to explain. It is easier to let things flow around you and only dive in if you see a dog to talk to, or maybe a stray potato chip (we still get to eat them if they are at someone else's house; we can't buy them ourselves). But I think it is a mistake to interpret this feeling as BAD. It really just is. Like everything else around us. We need to acknowledge that it is crap, and then we can continue shaking shit out, and hearing about everyone else and eating vegan burgers (we do this, and we like them – teamed with the bad hair and the lack of pants, I am getting a disturbing picture of the New Us). We also need lots of space. Shaking it out is hard work and involves a fair amount of flailing, both verbal and other. So that's it. Space. Acknowledgement. Recognition. And you might need to duck.

My Girl

Our daughter's birthday was just weeks after Oscar left. We celebrated it with family. We even sang, which we don't normally do, but it was the least awkward choice at the time. Weeks later, I found her birthday presents, stashed in my room in a previous life, and gave them to her.

It will soon be a year since Oscar chose his alternate reality and gave us this one. Colder days are a physical reminder of what is to come and what has passed. We have that day, then we have Oscar's birthday, then we have Bene's birthday. A daunting package of forty-four sleeps. We have scrambled to work out what to do when those days happen. We are nervous, angry, scared, devastated.

Bene is a gift. Even when the kids were small, we used to say (not even joking) that she was the reward we received to counter the trauma of having Oscar. Our family of four was always dominated by Oscar. He was the first child, the loudest, the most demanding. Bene learned very early to stick her elbows out when she needed to. She was not influenced by Oscar, but went her own way, a subtle and determined force. But all of us were overshadowed by Oscar. Who has now left.

It is April again. Soon Bene will be fifteen, having survived an unimaginably hard year. And as I tried to think of careful, kind, meaningful things to do in the upcoming days, I realised what we know, but because we are still learning this life, we keep screwing up.

We miss Oscar. And we want to remember him and cling to the time we had him physically present in our lives. But he's not here. And he doesn't need us now.

I think of what motivates us to get out of bed, to eat, to occasionally wash our hair and to keep our jobs. What makes seeing beauty in the world an essential part of each day. Why we look for recipes and try new foods. Why we go to the gym (the gym!). The one thing that drives all those efforts is Bene.

Bene is HERE, with us, being funny, confounding, energetic, thinking laterally, and essentially challenging – and trouncing – this reality like a pro. She's trying new things, making thoughtful gifts for friends, punching through her schoolwork, helping us and making our days 10000000000000 times better.

We talk about ways to remember Oscar. And that's good. But sometimes those conversations drown out what really needs to be said and remembered every day also. I look at the year that has passed, I think our daughter – suddenly an only child, now the oldest, now the recipient of our entire (sometimes manic) attention – deserves recognition. You know the meme that has a picture of a person and says, "This is Bene. Be like Bene."? I want that. Maybe as a T-shirt.

Being like Bene means being brave and being awesomely capable, even when scared. It means paying attention, and caring for others, even when every day you remember that this world sucks. It means still having the ability to laugh at the crappiest times in the world. It means being creative. It means astonishing insight. It means getting up every day and engaging, although the universe has entirely failed to show you a good reason why you should keep doing that.

Overwhelmingly, Bene is kind. I think of her when people say inappropriate or awkward things to me. She will say, "They just don't understand," or "They are trying to be nice." Sometimes she says, "What the fuck?" and we laugh.

Next week, our forty-four days begin. But I know what to do. When it's cold outside and, once again, we don't know what to say, and neither do you, we can talk about My Girl.

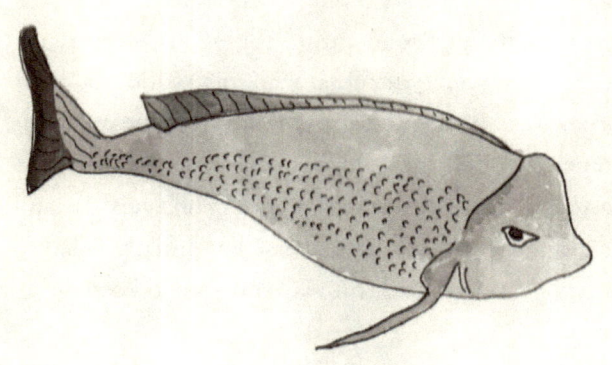

50 Ways to Leave Your Lover

So we're feeling pretty low – so low that country music is now part of the equation. To clarify this song choice, substitute the word life, for lover. And not in a suicidal way, just in a making changes way. I think we can make changes now. We kind of have to.

Frustratingly, we are now dealing with depression. As if my entire life of self-sufficiency was secretly generating a huge deficit of neediness and now I have to pay up. I hate needy people. I don't like over-sharers. I don't like people who cry too much. I don't like people who tell you terrible things randomly, when you don't know them and you have your own shitty day to deal with. I used to not like hugging though over the past year I have pushed through that one with friends and family (Dave – I'm talking about you. We hug now). I still don't like strangers touching me or standing too close.

I really don't like being the person with the saddest story, trumping anyone else's hard times with my own. It feels like a strange sort of terrible one-up-man-ship. Like, in the card game of life I am the queen of spades. Wearing a nice mask say, the two of hearts. But if pushed, I'm going to show my hand and it is *really* ugly (for reference, this card game is called Hearts).

Accepting all of our varied mental states has been the way we have travelled through the last year. I dislike this current version of us. Because we are so sad. And we cry all the time. And we can't see an end or a better time. I'm tired of needing people. I'm sick of asking my friends for their time. But we still need help. There must be something we can do to help ourselves, surely?

Psychologists. Check. Doctors. Check. Exercise. Check. Food. Check. Work. Check. Friends. Check. Self-care. Check. Accepting that grief takes time. Fucking Check.

Recently, I was told, "If you are really concerned, you can go up to the John Hunter and check in. There is a special place…" For suicidal people I guess, though, as always, the word suicide is like the word Voldemort. Nobody will say it. Even to us.

But there does not seem to be a middle ground. You are either coping in all its ugliness, at home, or you are tucked up in hospital. Mary Poppins would be good at this point. Or a spinster aunt, who turns up in times of trouble and feeds everyone broth and starches the laundry.

The fact is, we all feel sorry for us. And we all accept that grief takes time and there is no wrong way to do things. But something has to change now. Bene has not been to school in three weeks. That sounds like such a short time, but for her, and for us, it is an eternity. Will she ever go back? Are we home schoolers now? We don't know. She is working through her feelings and school is not compatible with that. So home it is.

And back to the 50 Ways. When reading the lyrics I was disappointed to find we are actually only given five ways. At this point they all sound good though. This week, we are slipping away to WA on a plane, not a bus. We are going to snorkel and swim with whale sharks. It sounds amazing but I have already adjusted my expectations to a picture where we are silent and weird on the boat full of people having "the experience of a lifetime!" I'm still keen.

Each day we try and come up with new plans for school, work, living, daily endurance… Mostly they get rejected, but on rare occasions one sticks.

Recently I accepted that I will never get back the control I once had to present myself a certain way. That me is gone. But also, I don't need to explain that to people. While in my head, I am presenting with a scary kabuki mask face, in reality, people are wonderfully unobservant. Maybe I seem a little strange, or a little dark or vague. Maybe not. I don't give a shit, and neither do they.

As an outside the house exercise, Bene and I have been attending open homes. The kind of houses you imagine would make you a different seeming person. They are over budget and impractical energy wise. They have amazing gardens and crazy tiles in all the wrong places. We talk about leaving our house for a while, and just being somewhere else to recalibrate ourselves. Pet sitting cats in Canada. Living in a secret garden in the country. Moving just around the corner because they have an awesome deck, and it is the Christmas lights street. Our home is still very firmly attached to our hearts and Oscar is here so we cannot let it go. However, a temporary change just may be acceptable.

We are still punching through our forty-four days and it is worse than I anticipated. Nobody wants to tell us what to do, because we seem so fragile, and so close to the edge. But we crave a plan or a simple set of steps to follow. Luckily, Paul Simon has our backs. Perhaps musically delivered direction will take off as a type of therapy? Self-guided and infinitely suited to all personality types. Cheap. Accessible. A New Plan. We're doing it.

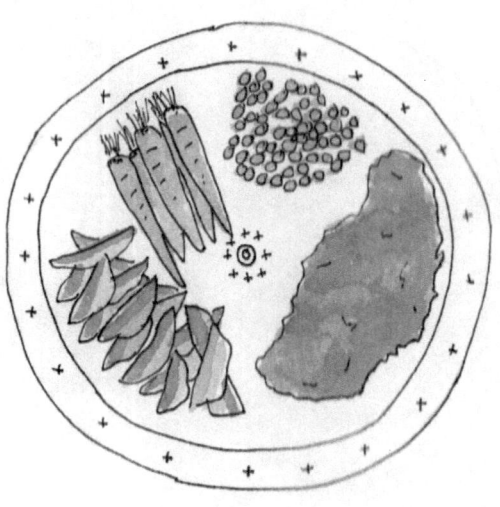

Mr Blue Sky

It is hard to hear this song without thinking of Megamind, but that's appropriate anyway. We have had a long, long period of being depressed and lack lustre, and you sort of feel like a Monster at those times. Simultaneously, as we have learnt to do, we are busting out and having fun and doing things with friends. So our last couple of months have been FUN, followed by Monster on couch, followed by PARTY, followed by Monster on couch under a blanket…

It is so hard to shift the mood that encompasses you when you know you are depressed but you cannot see – even though logically you know – that there is something different to follow. You're angry at yourself. You're angry at each other. You're ashamed that despite the huge amount of support and help you have, and people to call, you cannot bear to call them and say, "I want to die today," because it just sounds so ungrateful. You understand Oscar's choice. You see why people cut themselves or indulge in various self-harms because words cannot express the pain you are in or the hideous way that you feel about yourself. You want it to Show. What is the polite way to express that you have reached your limits and that you are scared that you will never feel any different? I do have a short list of people I can call, and I do, but some days – the Monster days – it is just better to turn the phone off, put that blanket on and stay warm. Dogs are a good addition to this scenario.

I feel like we should be wiser. I should have better and solemn words to say on trucking on through grief. But the recipe appears to actually be: Just keep doing stuff. Any stuff.

I quit my job due to necessity and the increase of time to think made me really doubt myself. I had more time to miss Oscar. I had more time to focus on Bene and worry about her. I wondered what I was doing with my life. I wondered if I had been faking being a superhero when, really, I was now going to just curl up on the floor and die, like so many people told me they would do. I started applying for different jobs and was suddenly faced with a need to explain why I left my old job that was palatable for people. I experimented with different ways to present myself. I imagined fake, shocking interview conversations that Oscar and I would have constructed and sniggered over.

In the end, I just told the truth (still looking for a job so I'll keep you posted as to whether this was the correct choice). It feels correct though. And at the same time, I kept on doing stuff, in between crapping out on the couch. I kept going to uni. We see old friends and new. I decided, while I was hating myself, I would combine this with another thing I hated and returned to the gym. I hate it, but today I am wearing a pair of previously too small underwear so, winning!

I guess what fascinates me is that I feel awful. I still sometimes expect Oscar to come home. I dreamed we were talking together the other night about our lives now, and woke physically curled up, in an agony of missing him. Bene and I have had some shocking days. We shout, and scream (me) and storm about the house in anger and sadness. It is almost unbearable.

But.

If you still get up the next day and do stuff, eventually you find yourself eating schnitzel and dancing with the dogs to Mr Blue Sky (while crying. just assume that everything you will be doing has crying somewhere in it). People have explained to me that the loss of Oscar is something that just becomes part of you as opposed to the gaping wound we normally feel. I couldn't picture it. Looking back at the last two months though, I wonder if this is what it looks like, a little bit. Storm. Storm. Storm. Blue Sky. Hopefully this ratio improves, but at least it is a picture that I can see.

Song list

Don't Be That Way
Ella Fitzgerald

Words
F.R. David

I've Got a Golden Ticket
Jack Albertson

B.I.N.G.O.
Royals

Out of Touch
Hall and Oates

You Can't Stop the Music
The Village People

My Favourite Things
Julie Andrews

Army of Me
Björk

Crazy
Grace Knight

The Bare Necessities
Phil Harris

Something is Not Right With Me
Cold War Kids

Spring, Spring, Spring
Jane Powell

Time After Time
Cyndi Lauper

I'm a Fantastic Wreck
Montaigne

Material Girl
Madonna

Shake it Out
Florence and the Machine

My Girl
The Temptations

50 Ways to Leave Your Lover
Paul Simon

Mr Blue Sky
ELO

www.ingramcontent.com/pod-product-compliance
Lightning Source LLC
Chambersburg PA
CBHW020327010526
44107CB00054B/2011